Mamá's Birthday Garden

by Isabella Stefan
Illustrated by Priscilla Burris

PEARSON

Glenview, Illinois • Boston, Massachusetts • Chandler, Arizona
Upper Saddle River, New Jersey

Paula used crayons to make a sign. Papá put strawberries on the cake. It was Mamá's birthday! This was going to be a special party.

The Ortiz family had just moved into their own house. They had always lived in a tiny apartment. They had never had a party in their own house before. This was going to be a special party!

Paula bounced with excitement.

Papá shook the soil from his gloves. "Are the flowers ready for planting?" he asked.

"Yes, the flowers are ready," Paula answered proudly. "I used all the money that I saved. This will be Mamá's best birthday ever."

---

soil: top layer of earth, dirt

"We need to work fast," Papá warned. "Mamá might get out of work early today."

Paula ran to get her wagon. "I have the flowers right here!" she said.

Papá could not believe his eyes. He stared at the flowers. They were plastic flowers!

"Oh, no! Plastic flowers!" he cried.

plastic flowers

wagon

What is wrong?" Paula asked. "These are just like the flowers Mamá had in our apartment. Mamá told me that one day we would have a garden. And she would plant flowers just like these!"

"Oh, Paula," Papá sighed.

Then Paula understood. She began to cry.

---

sighed: said slowly, with a sad or tired sound

Paula was crying at the back fence. She noticed Mrs. Bailey's beautiful flower garden next door. Just then, Mrs. Bailey came out. "What is the matter, Paula?" she asked.

Paula told her. "I bought plastic flowers for Mamá's garden. Now I have no more money and no real flowers!" she sobbed.

"Come with me," said Mrs. Bailey. "I have a plan."

Paula followed Mrs. Bailey. Mrs. Bailey explained her plan. Paula smiled. "The flower seeds are a great idea!" she said.

Then they got to work. Just as they finished, Mamá got home.

flower seeds

Mamá smiled when she saw the garden. "This is my best birthday ever!" she said. "Thank you, Paula!"

"Thank Mrs. Bailey," said Paula. "She gave me the flower seeds. The plastic flowers show what we planted. You will have flowers just like these, Mamá!"